A FOUNDATION OF STRUGGLES

OVERCOMING THE HURDLES OF LIFE, AND STEPPING INTO PURPOSE

EVANGELIST CHAVIS O. FRATER

Published by:

ISBN: 978-1-965635-06-3 (paperback)

Dedication

This book is dedicated to my only parent, Sereta Frater-Oakley, who is loving, caring, and supportive of me.

Thanks for bearing the shame and rejection for me and with me.

Many have said all manner of things about you when you were pregnant with me, but you didn't allow that to get the best of you. You have invested so much in my life.

Thank you, Mother.

I give honor to the Lord Jesus Christ for my life.

Thank You, Lord.

Prelude

From a tender age, my mother was brilliant in all she did but was treated unfairly at home. From about nine years old, she was sent to sleep at her grandmother's house to prevent her from being sexually assaulted by a family member, who attempted many times while she slept. During those nights, she was slapped by her mother in her sleep. She slapped her and repeated, *"Sleep properly. Sleep properly. Close up your feet."* She was scared because, as a child, she wouldn't know how to maintain closed legs during sleep.

This act of wickedness disturbed her life mentally. Later, she wanted to go where her father lived. In short order, she went to live with her father and stepmother. Her father was mostly out of town, which left her vulnerable to numerous abusive episodes by her stepmother. At the age of twelve, she was poisoned but she survived. She was then sent to stay with a female friend of her father's when he was away. When her father returned, she went home, but the rivalry continued.

She was associated with being abused until she thought of committing suicide. The power of almighty God held her in His hands and kept that spirit away from her. Thank You, Jesus, my mother has been through countless, sleepless nights with her pillows filled with tears. She was so ashamed to share her problems with anyone because she was scared that more disgrace would have been added to it. At that time, she failed to trust or to let anyone into her story...until now.

Acknowledgments

There are so many who contributed to the completion of this book through their love, support, inspiration, and the mark they made on my life. I am unable to list everyone who has contributed to my story by name. But I would like to express my deepest gratitude to you all.

Firstly, to Jesus Christ, my Lord and Saviour. I truly thank You for dying for my sake and fighting for me even when I did not realize it.

To my dear mother and friend, Sereta N. Frater-Oakley, from my heart, I truly say thanks for bearing the shame, pain, and rejection when you were pregnant with me. Thank you for not aborting me and, by extension, the purpose within me. Thank you. I love you, Mom.

To Monifa Frater, my lovely wife, confidant, and prayer partner. I want to express my heartfelt love and gratitude for the endless care, support, wisdom, and selfless service that you continue to extend to me in all areas of my life. I love you so much, my girl.

To my great-grandmother, Mercedes Dann, who left this life in July 2014 to be with the Lord. Thank you for the relationship we had. You have fought a good fight in my life and you did your best in helping to shape me into the man I have become. Thank you, Granny.

To my grandmother, St. Eleanor Skeel, you never said no when asked to keep me when I was a baby so my mother could work. You took the best care of me, your first grandson. Thank you for all you have done in my life.

I also want to express my deepest gratitude to my aunts, uncles, and cousins.

To Bishop Junior Purboo, my spiritual father. Thank you for your patience, understanding, and kindness towards me. I thank you specially for the word of knowledge that you have spent time to hand down to me. Thank you even for the exposure you have given to me. Blessings to your family from mine.

To Pastor Joan Rose-Perry, my spiritual mother. You were directly sent by God to be in my life. My life has taken a shift ever since we met. The calling that is upon my life gained a deeper stirring since you came into my life. Thank you for loving me as your own.

To all who have helped to shape me into the man I am today, I thank you. God placed so many of you in my life at strategic points to foster my growth and development. I would not be the person I am today without you. May God bless you all richly.

To those who will read this book, may you gain insights from my story and strength to endure and appreciate the difficult seasons that may come your way.

About the Author

Evangelist Chavis Frater is a vibrant young man from the parish of Clarendon. He accepted Jesus Christ as his personal saviour at the age twelve. He lives by the motto "Do your best, and God will do the rest."

He is a graduate of the New Covenant Bible Institute (now NCBIC), where he obtained a Diploma in Christian Leadership. He is also a past student of the Edna Manley College of Visual and Performing Arts where he obtained a certificate in Music Education.

He has served in the areas of Leadership Development, Prayer and Intercession, Youth Ministry, and Music Ministry. Though he enjoys working in these areas, his passion is to win souls for the kingdom of God through Evangelism. He believes that he could use the difficulties he faced in life as a stepping stone, not because of his resilience but because of God's faithfulness. To this end, he witnesses to souls that they too will come to know the God he calls saviour.

Foreword

The main purpose of this book is to highlight how to overcome the hurdles of life and how those who read it can step into their purpose.

Mr. Frater speaks about the effectiveness of single parenting and the importance of not living in denial regarding the heartaches, pain, and disappointments the role carries. He alluded to the fact that life is a teacher, presenting itself as a series of challenges while filling his mind with countless thoughts, questions, disappointments, and the price he should be willing to pay.

Mr. Frater further implored his reading audience not to become overwhelmed by the pressure and uncertainty of life itself. Living below one's potential and purpose should never become a choice (see 3 John 1:2).

The content of this book has influenced my thoughts towards individuals who become easily overwhelmed, and for certain, his audience will experience the same.

Chavis begins the book by sharing his mother's pain that brought him to a turning point, to journey with her faith and the godly, spiritual foundation she had built for him. It is this foundation that became the bedrock upon which his life would begin to change, thereby forging a path for Chavis to prayerfully put pen to paper to encourage us, his reading audience, to journey through the pages of this book, believing we will all experience a life-transforming encounter with "A Foundation of Struggles."

Apostle Andrew E. Green

Founder of Proclaim Ministries Int'l

Table of Contents

Chapter One

The Fatherless

And, "I will be a Father to you, and you will be my sons and daughters, says the Lord Almighty." (2 Corinthians 6:18 - NIV).

In the early years of my life, a question lingered in my heart, casting a shadow over the small joys of childhood: Where was the man I was supposed to call "Dad"? It wasn't as if I had even seen him in passing or heard his voice over the phone. There was no figure standing at the doorway when I returned from school, no warm embrace or deep voice guiding me through my early days. I couldn't help but notice that while my friends and cousins had fathers who played integral roles in their lives, I had no one to fill that space.

This absence gnawed at me, especially during moments when I saw my friends playing with their dads or heard them talking about their family trips. I remember trying to piece together what a father might be like. I'd imagine him tall, with strong arms that could lift me high, but no matter how vivid my imagination became, the reality was that I had never experienced what it felt like to have a father in my life. It was a mystery, one that weighed on me even as a child.

Eventually, curiosity and sadness pushed me to ask my mother the question I had been holding in for what felt like years. "Where is my father?" I asked one day, my voice trembling with both hope and fear. The look on her face stopped me in my tracks. Tears welled up in her eyes, and before she could say anything, the tears fell. I didn't know what to do. I had never seen her cry like this before, and it overwhelmed me. Without even thinking, I began to cry too. The room was filled with our sobs, an unspoken pain connecting us in that moment.

Once we regained our composure, my mother turned to me with a sad, weary look. I could see the weight of my question pulling at her. "My son," she began, her voice thick with emotion, "I don't even know where to begin." She paused, and it felt as though time had stopped. I waited, heart pounding, knowing that whatever she said next would change everything I thought I knew.

And then she began. She told me that when she was just a girl, living with her father and stepmother, something terrible had happened. One evening, her stepmother had sent her to the shop, a task that might have seemed ordinary on the surface but would turn into a nightmare. My mother, only fourteen at the time, was walking alone when three men saw her. At first, they merely walked alongside her, but as they reached a more isolated part of the road, their true intentions revealed themselves.

Without warning, one of the men grabbed her, covering her mouth so she couldn't scream. The other two grabbed her arms, and they dragged her into the bushes nearby. I listened in stunned silence as my mother described how one of them raped her while the others groped her body and violated her sense of safety. My mind struggled to comprehend the horror she had endured. She was only a child herself, and she had been forced to experience something no one, let alone a young girl, should ever have to face.

I couldn't stop myself from asking, "Did you still go to the shop after that?" My mother shook her head, her voice barely above a whisper as she said, "No." The weight of her experience hung heavy in the room, as though the walls themselves were absorbing the pain of her story. I pressed on, wanting to understand how she had survived such an ordeal. "What did your stepmother say when you came back late and without the items?"

Her stepmother, she told me, was furious. She cursed my mother, yelling at her for being slow and for not completing the errand as expected. My mother, who had just endured unimaginable trauma, was met with anger instead of compassion. Her stepmother's cruel words cut into her like a knife, adding insult to injury. She had always been the outsider in her stepmother's eyes, the child who didn't belong.

My mind raced. Where was her father during all of this? How could he not be there to protect her? When I asked, my mother explained that he was a businessman, often away for weeks or even months at a time. He had what she called "a wandering spirit," leaving home without a second thought and sometimes not returning for long stretches.

When my mother's pregnancy was discovered, her stepmother's disdain reached new heights. She, along with others in the community, urged my mother to get an abortion. At just fourteen, my mother didn't even know what an abortion was. She borrowed a dictionary from a neighbour, and once she learned what it entailed, she made a decision that would change both our lives— she refused to end the pregnancy.

This choice came with heavy consequences. Her stepmother, outraged that my mother had chosen to keep the baby, told her she could no longer stay in their house. So, at fourteen, my mother was left homeless, pregnant, and alone. She found refuge with strangers, people who were kind enough to take her in when her own family had turned their backs on her. I can't imagine how terrified she must have felt, navigating a world that had already been so unkind to her.

At the age of fifteen, my mother gave birth to me while still living with those strangers. She had no choice but to find work as a domestic helper to support us. Her first job paid just JM$100 a week, barely enough to survive, but she took whatever work she could find. She moved from one job to the next, enduring mistreatment and always searching for better opportunities to provide for us.

When I was three weeks old, my mother made the difficult decision to visit her own mother, my grandmother, in the parish of Clarendon. Up until that point, my grandmother had no idea that my mother had been pregnant, let alone that she had given birth. The news came as a shock, but over time, my grandmother and the rest of the family grew to accept me. My mother, needing to continue working, left me in my grandmother's care so that I could have some stability.

Living with my grandmother had its challenges, but the family eventually grew to love me. I became a part of their lives, even as my mother continued to work tirelessly to support both myself and her siblings. Every visit from her was a source of joy. She would marvel at how much I had grown, proud of the little milestones I reached, no matter how small.

I was told that my mother was undergoing severe and consistent warfare when she was pregnant. The pregnancy was under spiritual attack. At about a year and six months after my mother gave birth, my head was soft to the point that it could not be touched. It was said when I was born that my brain was not properly developed, and it was not guaranteed that I would be able to function as a normal baby.

By the time I started basic school, my mother's pride in me was palpable. She was overwhelmed with joy to see

22

me taking those first steps toward education. However, that joy was soon overshadowed by concern when it became apparent that I was not speaking. Around the age of four, my relatives noticed that while other children my age were beginning to form words and sentences, I remained silent. This realization broke my mother's heart. She took time off from work to stay with me, desperate to see any sign of progress.

During this time, my mother noticed that the tip of my tongue was fastened to the floor of my mouth. She pointed this out to nurses at the local Health Centre who referred me to the hospital. She was given dates for surgery, but each time it would be postponed. Though overwhelmed by the fact that I was not meeting such an important milestone, my mother kept on trusting the Lord for a miracle.

One faithful Saturday morning, and two days before my next scheduled surgery date, in a fit of misery, I began to cry uncontrollably. My mother rushed to my side and noticed something strange—there was blood in my mouth, specifically under my tongue. Upon closer inspection, she realized that the string beneath my tongue, which had been preventing me from speaking, had finally loosened. From that moment on, I was able to form simple words and, later, speak fluently.

As I continued to grow, my mother made every possible sacrifice to ensure I had what I needed. She worked long hours, often going without to make sure I was happy and comfortable. But despite all her efforts, there was one question that continued to weigh on my heart: who was my father?

I asked my mother if she had ever tried to find him or learn his name. She told me that she had heard people call him "Steve," but she wasn't sure if that was his real name. He and the other men who had assaulted her were strangers, working on a construction site in the area at the time. She had no way of knowing anything more about him.

This lack of information was difficult to accept. Growing up without a father left a void in my life that no amount of love from my mother could fill. Yet, even though I struggled with that absence, I knew my mother was struggling too. She battled depression, weighed down by the challenges of raising me on her own.

There were moments when the pressure became too much for her, and she would break down, overwhelmed by the weight of single parenting. She often vented her frustrations, recalling her own childhood and the ways in which she felt her parents had failed her. Sometimes, when I brought home poor grades from school or couldn't complete my assignments, she would lash out, not just with words but with physical punishment. The beatings were hard, and I feared them, but I also understood that they were the result of her pain.

High school brought its own set of challenges. I was still a slow learner, and no matter how hard I tried, I couldn't keep up with the pace of my classes. Teachers dictated lessons, and I couldn't write fast enough to capture everything. Eventually, they placed me in a slower class, but the shame of being left behind weighed heavily on me. At one point, the only words I could confidently spell were my three names and my mother's three names. The humiliation was unbearable.

People began to criticize me, saying that I was wasting my mother's time and money. They suggested that she stop sending me to school altogether. Report card day became a source of dread. I knew that my grades would only bring more disappointment, and the thought of facing my mother's anger filled me with anxiety.

Yet, despite all these challenges, my mother never gave up on me. She fought for me every step of the way, sacrificing her own needs to ensure that I had a chance at success. Through her perseverance, I learned the value of resilience—the idea that it's not about how many times we fall but about how many times we get back up.

The most important lesson I've learned through all of this is that, even though my earthly father was absent, I have a Heavenly Father who has never abandoned me. The circumstances of my birth may not have been ideal, but I refuse to let them define me. God has always watched over me, and I take comfort in knowing that His eyes are always on the fatherless and the orphaned. He is the Father to the fatherless, and in Him, I have found my identity.

Chapter Two

The Rejected One

After I sat the Grade Six Achievement Test (GSAT), I was excited to know which high school I had passed for. However, when the results came, the school I was assigned to was far beyond my reach, geographically and financially. It wasn't just the distance that was the issue; my mother was working in Kingston as a live-in domestic helper, meaning she wouldn't be able to take care of me while also maintaining her job. The situation felt hopeless, and I could see the worry etched on my mother's face. She knew I needed an education, but the circumstances were stacked against us.

Fortunately, my mother's uncle—my granduncle—heard about our situation. He knew that my mother needed someone to take care of me while she continued to work to provide for both of us. My granduncle, living near the high school, offered to keep me at his house so that I could attend school. He promised my mother that I would be well looked after. My mother, relieved and grateful, agreed to the arrangement. She would come to visit me every two weeks while I lived with my granduncle and his family.

At first, living with my granduncle's family seemed like a solution to all our problems. I started school and gradually settled into my new environment. It wasn't easy being away from my mother, but I told myself that this was the best option for my future. I tried my best to adapt to living with my relatives, and initially, they were welcoming enough. However, as time went on, I noticed subtle changes in their behaviour. It was like the atmosphere in the house began to shift, and the warmth I had felt at the beginning slowly dissipated.

One of the first signs that things were changing was when I realized that my sleeping arrangements were becoming a point of contention. When I first moved in, my granduncle had arranged for one of his sons, my cousin, to sleep at his grandmother's house next door so that I could have a place to sleep in their house. For about two weeks, my cousin would leave at night to stay with his grandmother, only to return in the mornings. It seemed like a fair arrangement, and I didn't think much of it at the time.

But soon after, things took a turn. My cousin, who had been going to his grandmother's house to sleep, started to make excuses about not leaving at night. He would wait until I had gone to bed, then wake me up, demanding that he needed to sleep in his bed. I had no choice but to gather the sheet my mother had given me and lie down on the cold, hard concrete floor. It was brutal, especially on nights when the cold crept in through the cracks in the walls. For the next two years, this would be the place I slept.

At one point, I mustered the courage to ask my granduncle for a piece of sponge to lie on. I couldn't bear the physical discomfort any longer. His response crushed me. He told me that I was a man now, and I needed to bear it. His words stung, but I didn't argue. I didn't tell my mother about the situation because I knew she would be devastated and angry. She had enough burdens to carry, and I didn't want to add to her worries.

Living with my granduncle's family was far from easy. They cooked three meals a day, but I only ever received one meal—dinner. Hunger became a familiar companion, and I learned to survive by drinking water throughout the day to stave off the gnawing emptiness in my stomach. Whenever they prepared meals, they would serve their children first, calling them by name to come and eat. By the time they remembered me, it was often too late. On most nights, after everyone else had eaten and gone to bed, my granduncle's wife would casually mention, *"Little boy, your dinner is in the kitchen."*

I'd go to the kitchen, my stomach growling, only to find that the food had been left uncovered, exposed to the ants, cockroaches, flies, and sometimes even rats that roamed the house. But I was too hungry to care. I ate the contaminated food, grateful for the little that I received, even though it made me feel more like a scavenger than a family member. God bless the little food they shared with me because even though it wasn't much, it kept me going.

Whenever they prepared ground provisions—bananas, yam, and dumplings—I was given the smallest portions. One finger of banana, a tiny piece of yam, one dumpling, and a single piece of meat. It was never enough. Even my youngest cousin, who was attending prep school, received larger portions than I did. One evening after church, we sat down for dinner, and when my granduncle saw the pitiful portion on my plate, he spoke up for the first time. *"Good God, man. You can do better than that,"* he told his wife. *"Put more food on his plate."*

Her response was sharp and bitter. *"You're not providing anything in this house,"* she snapped, making it clear that his words carried no weight. My granduncle fell silent, and so did I. After that, I never expected anything to change.

One of the most humiliating experiences I faced while living there happened around the dinner table. After collecting my dinner one evening, I joined my cousins at the table, thinking nothing of it. But when my granduncle's wife saw me sitting with her children, her face twisted in anger. She stormed over, grabbed my plate, and hurled it onto the floor. *"You should never sit around my table again,"* she hissed. From that day forward, I never sat at their table again.

The constant hunger was wearing me down, so I asked my mother if she could buy me some snacks. She did, and I thought I had finally found a small solution to my problem. I asked my granduncle if I could store the snacks in the kitchen cupboard, but he shrugged and said, *"Ask my wife."* When I asked her, she refused, telling me to keep the snacks in my room instead. I didn't think much of it at the time, but soon after, I noticed that the snacks were disappearing. I asked my cousins if they had been taking them, but they denied it, accusing me of eating the snacks myself and pretending otherwise.

Things continued to deteriorate. The house itself was unfinished. We washed plates and used the bathroom outside. At night, my cousins would urinate in a bath and leave it there in the unfinished bathroom inside. Every morning, I was the one expected to empty the urine, though I did not use it. One day, I refused to take the urine out. I was tired of being taken advantage of. My granduncle confronted me, accusing me of being the one responsible for the mess. I told him firmly that it wasn't me and I wasn't going to clean it up. He beat me with a broad belt, and I shouted through the pain, *"You'll have to kill me today because I'm not taking it out."*

Later that night, my granduncle discovered that it was actually his son who had been urinating in the bath all along. His son had been lying the entire time, allowing me to take the blame. When my granduncle confronted him, the truth finally came out. Yet, despite being proven right, it didn't change how they treated me. My granduncle's wife remained indifferent, and my cousins' behaviour grew even more unpredictable. One minute they were kind, and the next, they were cruel.

The most terrifying incident happened when one of my cousins decided he wanted to get rid of me. He came into the room one day, acting unusually nice, asking if I had any snacks left. I told him I did, and then, without warning, he pulled out a gun and pointed it at me. I stood there, frozen, as he threatened to kill me if I ever told his parents anything about him again. I was terrified, and that fear stayed with me for a long time.

There were other dangerous moments as well. One night, I woke up to the smell of gas and heat. My cousin had set the house on fire. We all rushed to put it out, and my granduncle chased him down and beat him. But that wasn't the end of it. On another occasion, my cousin came to the workshop where I was working with my granduncle, brandishing an offensive weapon and threatening to kill both of us. Life with these relatives was like living in a war zone, never knowing when the next attack would come.

Despite all of this, my granduncle had no shame in asking me for money. He would come to me on Wednesdays or Thursdays, flashing a smile and asking if he could borrow some cash until the weekend. I always lent him the money, but he never paid it back. One weekend, I desperately needed the money to buy soap powder to wash my clothes. When I asked him for it, he brushed me off, and I never saw that money again.

It wasn't until my mother came to visit unexpectedly that I realized just how rejected I had been. She travelled all the way from Kingston because her heart and mind were troubled, and she needed to see me. When she arrived, she found me sitting outside, alone, hungry, and worried about how I would wash my clothes. My cousins' clothes were already hanging on the line to dry, while I had nothing.

When I told her everything, my mother broke down in tears. From the moment I was conceived, I had been a rejected child—rejected by my father, my relatives, and even life itself. But my mother, despite her own struggles, always stood by me. She bought me food, left some for me, and returned to work, her heart heavy with the knowledge of the mistreatment I was enduring.

Life with my granduncle's family was harsh and unforgiving. I wasn't just rejected—I was neglected, mistreated, and abused. My smallest cousin once hit me in the eye with a piece of board, leaving me in pain for days. When I complained to his father, his mother intervened, defending her son and blaming me for the incident.

Church, once a place of joy when I attended with my mother, became another source of pain when I went with my relatives. Their behaviour at church didn't match how they treated me at home. They acted like the most righteous people in the congregation, but I knew the truth. I often sat alone in a corner, reflecting on the hypocrisy I witnessed.

School wasn't much better. One day, while sitting in class, someone reached through the hole in a block wall and snatched my pen. I ran out to confront the person, only to find my cousin approaching. I felt a surge of confidence, thinking he would defend me. But I was wrong. He sided with the other boy—his cousin from his mother's side—and slammed my forehead into the sharp edge of the wall. Blood sprayed everywhere. I was rushed to the nurse's office, where they told me I could have died if the blow had been just an inch closer to my brain.

I received eight stitches that day. When I returned home and told my granduncle and his wife what had happened, they showed no concern. This marked the end of my stay with my granduncle and his family. My mother came for me and took me to the doctor. I had multiple visits to the doctor after that, but my mother had to bear this burden alone. They didn't ask my mother how she was managing or offered any help with my recovery.

The scar from that incident remains on my face to this day—a permanent reminder of the rejection and suffering I endured while living with those relatives. Life with them was far from a walk in the park; it was a daily battle for survival, both physically and emotionally.

Chapter Three

The Rugged Life

After that incident, my mother decided never to leave me with anyone again. She had to leave the job she was accustomed to and find another source of income so I could live with her permanently. I was also moved to a different high school, which would be more affordable and provide a new environment.

During this period, I was nurtured in a way that had become unfamiliar. Life with my mother was good, and my experience at my new high school was quite amicable. I had many challenges but this was dim in comparison to the deep joy I had being with my mom.

I still had significant challenges learning the concepts that were being taught. When I left high school, my average was a shockingly low 0.49. It was a moment of harsh realization—life's reality hit me like a tidal wave. How was I supposed to survive in the world with such an abysmal academic record? This realization triggered a deep fear in me that I wasn't sure how to overcome. But despite the odds stacked against me, there was something that had been planted deep within me that would become my lifeline—my mother's faith and the godly, spiritual foundation she had built for me. That foundation would be the bedrock upon which my life would begin to change.

Because of the godly upbringing my mother had given me, I found myself in circles with others who were far more intelligent, talented, and well-educated than I was. At first, I felt overwhelmed and out of place. I couldn't help but feel intimidated, constantly worried about what others would say or think if I stumbled or made mistakes. When I heard other boys reading with such ease, the gulf between their abilities and mine felt insurmountable. Yet, instead of letting this discourage me, it sparked a small flame of hope within me. Philippians 4:13 became my anchor: *"I can do all things through Christ who strengthens me."*

I held on to that verse during moments when doubt threatened to swallow me whole. Though I often felt insecure and wondered if I would ever measure up, being around these individuals taught me something crucial: life was a journey, and everyone's progress was a work in progress. The success I longed for wouldn't come overnight but through perseverance and faith.

As I spent more time with friends at church, things started to shift in my life. I was no longer just sitting on the sidelines; I was getting more involved. Slowly but surely, I began to participate in church activities. Every time I was called upon to do something, whether it was reading a passage of scripture or helping with an event, I grew a little stronger. What once terrified me now became a source of growth. The more I stepped forward, the more confident I became, and the fear of embarrassment started to fade away.

It wasn't just my participation that grew—it was my understanding. I began to believe that perhaps I could become brilliant, too. I started picking up the Bible daily and skipping through. One day, while looking through the Bible, I came upon the word 'Forasmuch.' At the time, I had not seen a word that seemed this long. I took the Bible to my mother and asked her to tell me the word. Instead, she pointed at me with a smile and said, " Yuh a read!" I felt encouraged, and with a smile on my face and in my heart, I caught that word deep in my spirit. I walked away knowing that I would read.

At first, my reading was slow and laborious. I struggled with the words, but I kept at it. With each passing day, my reading improved, little by little. I wasn't just reading for the sake of it, though; I was learning, absorbing, and growing spiritually. The more I immersed myself in the Word of God, the more mature I became—not only in my faith but in every aspect of my life.

The transformation taking place in my life was evident to those around me. One of the first major opportunities to demonstrate the inner change I was experiencing came when I was asked to expound on a scripture in children's church. It was a small step, but it felt monumental to me. That small act of sharing a scripture evolved into being asked to speak in front of the congregation during Sunday night services. At first, I was terrified. My presentations were not based on my own knowledge but on the lessons I had absorbed through Sunday School and Bible Study. The foundation of faith my mother had laid for me was beginning to bear fruit.

In addition to my growing spiritual involvement, I found myself drawn to music, particularly the drums. I would spend hours watching the more experienced drummers play during Sunday morning services. Their skill captivated me, and I longed to learn how to play. I began playing around with the drumset when no one was watching, practicing on my own, even though I wasn't nearly as skilled as the others. When the main drummers didn't show up on time, I was the one who filled in. I could feel the congregation's mixed reactions—some people were supportive, while others clearly weren't.

I'll never forget one Sunday morning when I was on my way to the music area to play the drums. A church sister saw me heading in that direction and openly called out, *"Little boy, if you want to learn to play the drums, let your 'mumma' send you to music school."* Her words stung, especially since others around her agreed, nodding or murmuring their approval. They all knew my mother didn't have the means to send me to music school, but I didn't let that stop me. I smiled at her, knowing in my heart that her words would not discourage me. I thought to myself, *"You won't stop me from playing the drums,"* and I continued on my way.

Years passed, and I persevered. I became a great drummer, playing at churches all around. One day, I sat back and reflected on how far I had come, remembering that woman's words and how she had tried to block my path. If I hadn't pushed through, if I had listened to her discouragement, I wouldn't have become the musician I was that day. Ironically, the same lady who had once told me to let my mother send me to music school was now the one asking me to play the drums whenever the regular musicians were unavailable. It reminded me of Psalm 118:22, *"The stone the builders rejected has become the cornerstone."* What others intended for harm, God used for good, just as He did in Genesis 50:20.

But my journey didn't end with music. There was a time when life felt stagnant; when nothing seemed to be happening for me. I watched as people around me moved ahead in life, advancing in their careers, relationships, and personal development, while I felt stuck. It was as though I was trapped in a cycle of rugged hardship, with little to no formal education to lean on.

To survive, I took on side jobs, working with tradesmen to help ease the financial burden on my mother. It wasn't easy. The physical labour took a toll on my young body, especially my back, which often ached from the strain. I was not yet mature enough for the heavy work I was doing, but I had no other option. I knew my mother needed me to contribute, so I pushed through the pain.

God, however, had other plans for me. In His own timing, He opened a new door. I heard about the Edna Manley College of the Visual and Performing Arts, specifically the School of Music. Though I had no resources to pursue such an education, God's favour found me. I enrolled at Edna Manley and completed my courses, earning a certificate in music education. It was a significant achievement, but even then, I knew that music was not the only calling God had placed on my life.

I began to sense a deeper calling into ministry. My former bishop and pastor also recognized this calling and encouraged me to stay faithful to God's will for my life. With their guidance, I started preaching in my local community, and soon, I was being invited to various congregations to share the Word of God.

As I grew in my ministry, I knew I needed to further equip myself. I enrolled in the New Covenant Bible Institute, where I studied theology and Christian

Leadership for two full years. The time I spent there was transformative. It helped me gain a deeper understanding of God's Word and prepared me to serve the church and the wider community more effectively. I graduated with a diploma, ready to step into the next phase of my calling.

After finishing Bible college, I returned to my church, eager to serve. But life took another unexpected turn. My passion for ministry began to wither as I encountered resistance from the very people I thought would support me. My pastor, who had once encouraged me, no longer seemed to see the effectiveness of my ministry. I noticed that I was no longer being asked to lead fasting or prayer meetings— roles I had once been excited to fill.

I couldn't help but wonder where I had gone wrong. Had I done something to upset my pastor or the other church members? I sought answers but found none. As time went on, it became clear that something had changed. The pastor was distant, and I felt as though I was being sidelined. When I received calls to minister at other churches, I always sought my pastor's permission and covering, but he often discouraged me, saying he didn't feel it in his spirit to send me.

It was a difficult season. I felt like the gift God had placed within me was going to waste. I had a calling to preach the Gospel, but every door seemed to be closing. I started questioning everything—had I misunderstood God's plan for my life? Was I truly meant to be an evangelist?

Despite the confusion, I sought the Lord in prayer and fasting. I needed His guidance more than ever. After more than a year of seeking, I finally received an answer. God had not abandoned me, and His plan for my life had not changed. With this assurance, I knew it was time to move forward.

I wrote a letter of resignation to my pastor, explaining my decision to leave the church. He read the letter aloud before the congregation one Sunday morning, and afterward, he called an urgent meeting. During the meeting, I shared my heart with the congregation, explaining what had been happening to me and why I felt it was time to move on. Some were shocked, others saddened, but most were understanding. A few accused me of leaving the church for money, but I knew in my heart that was far from the truth.

Even though the transition was difficult, I remained humble. I continued attending services until the date specified in my letter, and the handover was smooth.

In the years that followed, I travelled across Jamaica to minister in various churches. There were times when I received no financial compensation, not even a bottle of water, but I continued to trust God to provide for me. I'll never forget the day a pastor called me to preach, and I honestly told him, *"I only have enough fare to get there, but not enough to get back."* He assured me that he would take care of it. After the service, however, he disappeared without a word. I stood outside under an ackee tree, unsure of how I would get home. I prayed and left it in God's hands. Miraculously, a woman from the church offered me a ride, and I made it home safely.

The rugged life had not broken me—it had only made me stronger.

Chapter Four

The Excruciating Period

T en years ago, I attended Bible study at my former church on a Thursday night. The assistant pastor was leading the session, as she often did. As I settled into my seat, I could sense the usual energy of mid-week services—a mixture of spiritual hunger and the routine comfort of familiar faces. The topic of discussion that night seemed like any other, until a senior member raised her hand to ask a question.

Her question was simple but profound: *"Can a man live his entire life in this world without sin?"* The room fell into a brief silence as everyone awaited the assistant pastor's response. She confidently answered, *"Yes, he can."* I immediately noticed a few quiet murmurs from the congregation, indicating some disagreement, but nothing was said out loud. I raised my hand, feeling compelled to ask the same question to clarify the matter.

When the assistant pastor acknowledged me, I repeated the question, *"Can a man truly live his entire life in this world without sin?"* She answered once again, *"Yes, you can."* Then I restated the question by saying, *"How can a man live his entire life in this world without sin?"* However, this time her husband, who was sitting in the audience, interjected forcefully. He stomped his foot and, with a tone of authority, said, *"By doing what the Word of the Lord says,"* his attitude clearly showed his impatience with my inquiry.

I wasn't satisfied with these responses, and I felt there was more to be discussed. So I began quoting scripture, starting with Ecclesiastes 7:20, which says, *"For there is not a just man upon earth, that doeth good, and sinneth not."* Then I followed it with Psalm 51:5, which states, *"Behold, I was shapen in iniquity; and in sin did my mother conceive me."* Despite presenting these verses, I still didn't feel like my concerns were being addressed adequately.

I tried to get the assistant pastor's attention again, calling her by her title, "Pastor," several times, but she ignored me. Frustrated, I called her by her name. Only

Chavis O. Frater

then did she finally respond, but her husband became furious. He stood up and admonished me, saying I should address his wife properly because she was the pastor of the church. I asked him why he hadn't said anything earlier when I addressed her by her title, and she didn't respond. His anger escalated as he replied, *"The law of the land gives me permission to gird up anyone misbehaving and put them out of the church."* He came closer to me, his face inches from mine, and declared that he would personally throw me out if necessary.

The tension in the room was thick. A few people spoke up, saying that his behaviour was uncalled for and that I hadn't done anything wrong, but the majority of the congregation remained silent. Most of them were clearly intimidated by the assistant pastor's husband, and it was evident that this wasn't the first time he had caused a scene.

I remained seated throughout the rest of the study session, not leaving until the Bible Study was officially dismissed. The entire episode left me feeling isolated and hurt, especially since some of the members who had witnessed everything did not speak up or offer support. I could sense the deep-rooted fear and respect the congregation had for the assistant pastor and her husband, but the lack of fairness cut me deeply.

That Sunday, the assistant pastor was in church, but something was off. She wasn't participating in the service as she usually did. Instead, she sat quietly, writing in a notebook throughout the entire service. When the bishop finished preaching, he announced that she had something to say and gave her the opportunity to address the congregation. I sat there, watching as she greeted everyone and began to explain the events of the Bible Study session. To my dismay, she twisted the situation to paint herself and her husband as the victims. She only shared part of the story—what I had said—but conveniently left out the things she and her husband had done and said to me.

When she finished speaking and returned to her seat, I could hear the congregation murmuring. They were upset, assuming that whoever had spoken against the assistant pastor was in the wrong. I raised my hand and asked the bishop if I could respond. He allowed me to speak, but just as I began explaining my side of the story, the bishop interrupted me. *"We need to stop this foolishness in God's house,"* he declared. His abruptness left me feeling silenced and unjustly treated.

I told him, *"You're not being fair. You allowed the assistant pastor to speak about the matter publicly, yet you're not giving me the same opportunity."* A few people in the congregation agreed with me, but most stayed silent, not wanting to get involved. The injustice of the situation weighed heavily on me. The hurt I felt was excruciating, not just because of the incident itself but because of the way the church leadership handled it. It felt like a deep betrayal from a place where I had sought spiritual refuge.

In the weeks that followed, I struggled with a bitterness that consumed me. I felt rejected by the very people who were supposed to be my spiritual family. The pain and unforgiveness festered in my heart, making it difficult for me to interact with the church members. I even contemplated reacting violently at times, but deep down, something inside me—perhaps the voice of the Holy Spirit—kept whispering, *"This too shall pass."*

Nights became especially difficult. I was afraid to sleep, haunted by the thought that if I died in my bitterness, I might lose my soul. I knew I was wrong to hold on to the anger, but letting go felt impossible. My heart was heavy, and I felt isolated from God because of the hardness that had settled inside me. People would ask me how I was doing, and I would respond honestly, *"I'm not okay. Church people are causing me pain."*

One day, while I was walking along the road, my spiritual father saw me and stopped his vehicle. He had heard about the incident and wanted to discuss it with me. He expressed his concern about my reaction to the church leadership and suggested that I make an open apology to the church. At first, I resisted the idea. I didn't believe I was the only one who needed to apologize. However, out of respect for him, I agreed to go before the church and apologize.

When I stood before the congregation and delivered the apology, my words felt hollow. I did it because I was asked to, not because I truly felt it in my heart. The bitterness still clung to me like a dark cloud. I thought the apology would resolve things, but it didn't bring the peace I was hoping for.

One late night, as I lay awake, the Holy Spirit began to speak to me. His voice was gentle yet firm, telling me that I needed to truly apologize—not just for the sake of appearances, but from a place of sincerity. I couldn't ignore it anymore. The next morning, I went to the pastor and told him that I wanted to offer a sincere apology to him and the congregation. He brushed it off, saying I was the only one holding on to the matter. But I insisted, telling him that I wasn't there to debate the issue, only to do what God had instructed me to do.

The pastor finally gave me the opportunity, and this time, I apologized from my heart. As I stood there, speaking the words I had resisted for so long, I felt the weight of the bitterness begin to lift. It wasn't an instant transformation, but I knew that by obeying the Holy Spirit, I had taken the first step toward healing.

Life has a way of teaching us painful lessons, and the journey toward forgiveness is often filled with bumps and setbacks. After the altercation at church, it took time for things to return to some semblance of normalcy. I could eventually see the assistant pastor and her husband without feeling the sting of anger in my heart, but the relationship was never the same.

According to Ephesians 4:31, *"Let all bitterness, and wrath, and anger, and clamor, and evil speaking, be put away from you, with all malice."* This verse became my guiding light during that season. Life may not always return to what it once was, but sometimes, the only way forward is to accept what has happened, let go of the past, and move on with grace.

Chapter Five

The Effects of Single Parenting

WHAT IS SINGLE PARENTING?

According to Merriam-Webster, a single parent is someone who lives with a child or children and no husband, wife, or partner. This can occur due to various circumstances, such as physical abuse, verbal abuse, financial abuse, divorce, separation, the death of a spouse, or a conscious decision to become a single parent.

A SINGLE MOTHER SPEAKS

Being a single teenage mother, I want to encourage you not to let your situation enslave you or make you feel fragile. Don't let the wear and tear of life or indecision prevent you from building the strong character you need. Embrace your journey and surround yourself with people who have your best interests at heart—not heartbreakers, users, or idlers. Stay focused and always remain aware that someone is entirely dependent on you to mould them into a person of worth.

Remember, being a single parent is hard work, full of challenges, trials, and frustrations, so you'll need a strong support system along the way. Never leave your child unprotected. Carefully choose trustworthy people to care for them while you're away, and be mindful—even relatives can sometimes become harmful or abusive. Create an environment of open communication with your child. Make sure they feel safe and free to share their experiences with you. Be your child's best friend—listen to them, understand their feelings, and let them know you care deeply.

Defend your child's rights and handle matters affecting them with respect. Be careful not to compare them to others or make them feel embarrassed. Spread love in everything you do—let it be seen and felt by your child every day.

One statement I always emphasize is this: **Put God First in Any and Every Situation.** I also want to encourage teenage girls who may become pregnant, whether by choice or circumstance: **DO NOT COMMIT ABORTION.** Your life and your child's life have immense value, and there is always hope for a brighter future.

Secondly, I would encourage young single parents to never give up on their child or children. Place great emphasis on Christian growth, morals, and ethics. Raise your children with love and instill in them positive values, even when life seems like a dead end, and hope feels distant. Do not give up. Always love your child or children. Be the motivator, mentor, and role model they need—be their hero. Celebrate your children in every little achievement they make, and create that same encouraging atmosphere for others, even when someone else's achievements seem more outstanding. Remember, the race is not over until it's over.

Finally, avoid discussing your child or children with negative people. Seek professional help where it's needed, and surround yourself and your child with positive, supportive influences.

— Sereta Frater-Oakley

WHAT DOES THE BIBLE SAY ABOUT SINGLE PARENTING?

Based on the principle of the scriptures, single parenting was never God's intention from creation. God intended for families to be together as one.

Genesis 2:18, "And the LORD God said, It is not good that the man should be alone; I will make him an help meet for him."

Genesis 2:24, *"Therefore shall a man leave his father and his mother, and shall cleave unto his wife: and they shall be one flesh."*

This is clear evidence that single parenting was never God's intention from creation.

According to Psalms 127:3, *"Lo, children are an heritage of the LORD: and the fruit of the womb is his reward." (KJV).*

It is clear from the scriptures that children are a gift from God, and they are chosen in Him even before the foundation of this world. In the Word of God, a child or children is not a mistake; it was a part of God's plan.

Deuteronomy 6:4-9, *"Hear, O Israel: The LORD our God is one LORD: And thou shalt love the LORD thy God with all thine heart, and with all thy soul, and with all thy might. And these words, which I command thee this day, shall be in thine heart: And thou shalt teach them diligently unto thy children, and shalt talk of them when thou sittest in thine house, and when thou walkest by the way, and when thou liest down, and when thou risest up. And thou shalt bind them for a sign upon thine hand, and they shall be as frontlets between thine eyes. And thou shalt write them upon the posts of thy house, and on thy gates."*

God was precise in telling the Israelites, His chosen people, to pass His law on to their children. The Israelites were a set of people whose lives centered around what they received from the Lord.

While growing up, there is an old saying that *"Children live what they learn,"* so it is imperative that our children are raised in an environment where God's Word is valued and shared.

Deuteronomy 6:7, *"And thou shalt teach them diligently unto thy children, and shalt talk of them when thou sittest in thine house, and when thou walkest by the way, and when thou liest down, and when thou risest up."*

The Merriam-Webster dictionary defines "diligently" as an adverb, and it means: actively, in a manner involving great or constant activity; as in hard, with great effort or determination.

From a Biblical perspective, "diligently" comes from the Hebrew Shânan (shaw-nan'); a primitive root; to point (transitive or intransitive); intensively, to pierce; figuratively, to inculcate:—prick, sharp(-en), teach diligently, whet.

EXAMPLES OF SINGLE PARENTS

According to 1 Kings 17:9-10, there was a woman who had been a single mother due to the death of her husband. Life had taken a different direction. Now, the principle of the Word is that a man is the breadwinner, which is one who earns money to support his family.

This woman's financial support had died leaving her with their son to take care of. She had reached the end of her rope and was gathering sticks to prepare their last meal and die. But, little did she know that the boy's Heavenly Father had seen and felt all they were going through. In all this calamity, God informed His servant, Elijah, that He had commanded a widow in Zarephath to sustain him. When Elijah came to the gate of the city, behold, the widow woman was there gathering sticks. He called to her and said, *"Fetch me, I pray thee, a little water in a vessel, that I may drink."*

And as she was going to fetch it, he called to her a second time and said, *"Bring me, I pray thee, a morsel of bread in thine hand. Take along with thee something to eat."* She replied, *"As the LORD thy God liveth, I have not a cake, but a handful of meal in a barrel, and a little oil in a cruse: and, behold, I am gathering two sticks, that I may go in and dress it for me and my son, that we may eat it, and die."*

Single parenting is not easy, but it is possible. The Lord, in all His mercy, cares, provides for, shelters and protects those who need Him. He is a father to the fatherless and the defender of the widows.

Whatever your situation may look like, God is well able. Like this woman who received bountiful provision during her famine, God will make a way during your crisis.

Chapter Six

Life is a Teacher

At first, life seemed utterly meaningless to me. I had no clear direction, no understanding of what I might become. Life presented itself as a series of challenges, filling my mind with countless thoughts, questions, and disappointments. I felt overwhelmed by the pressure and uncertainty of it all, to the point where I began living far below the potential and purpose that the Word of the Lord had laid out for me.

3 John 1:2 says, *"Beloved, I wish above all things that thou mayest prosper and be in health, even as thy soul prospereth." (KJV).*

This was a promise from God for my life, yet in those early days, I couldn't see how it applied to me. My mind was clouded with doubts about my future, and I was unable to recognize the value of my own existence.

In the community where I grew up, few people excelled academically, financially, or even spiritually. The way of life revolved around farming and chicken rearing, which were the main sources of livelihood for many families. Education was not seen as a primary means of advancement, and outside of school, there were few voices encouraging the pursuit of academic success. The lack of role models or mentors meant that most children, including myself, didn't see a future beyond the boundaries of our small community.

For me, attending school was just a routine. Monday to Friday, I went because my mother made sure I was there. She always left or sent enough money to cover my school fees and expenses. But even though I physically attended school, my mind wasn't engaged. School life was not a joy for me; it was a source of pain, frustration, and constant questioning. Why wasn't I able to grasp the lessons? Why couldn't I retain what was being taught? I listened to the teachers, but inside my head, it was a battle. Learning didn't come naturally to me. My brain seemed to struggle and fight against every piece of information I tried to process.

From a young age, I realized that the very mention of "books" caused me anxiety. As soon as someone tried to talk to me about studying or schoolwork, my whole being seemed to crumble. My mind simply wasn't equipped to handle academic learning in the same way other children could. It wasn't that I didn't want to succeed—I desperately wanted to—but my brain didn't seem strong enough to win the fight.

Looking back, I can now recognize that I was dealing with mental and emotional struggles that contributed to my inability to learn as I should have. The challenges I faced, the neglect, and the emotional trauma all played a role in shaping my cognitive abilities. These experiences left deep scars, but they also taught me some of life's most valuable lessons.

Everyone has a story to tell, and each narrative is different. I believe that sharing our stories holds incredible power. When we share our struggles and triumphs, we provide hope for others who may be facing similar challenges. Hope, in itself, is a powerful currency—it can help a person endure even the harshest of realities. The most important thing to remember is that no matter what we are going through, we are never truly alone.

Today, I am tremendously blessed in so many ways. I have experienced significant spiritual growth and have been given the opportunity to touch many lives. I am now able to learn challenging things easily and figure things out without explanation. The wisdom of the Lord continues to guide me in all areas of life. The things that seemed out of reach in the past are now within my grasp.

Life has taught me many profound lessons, and I want to share these lessons in the hope that they will serve as stepping stones for your own elevation in life. My experiences have been filled with hardship, neglect, and emotional trauma, but they also provide powerful lessons that I believe anyone can draw from.

RESILIENCE IN THE FACE OF ADVERSITY

Life can be overwhelmingly difficult, especially when rejection comes from the very people who are supposed to care for you. My journey taught me that resilience is one of the most valuable traits we can cultivate—the ability to endure hardship and not allow it to define who we are. Despite being mistreated, neglected, and even abused, I found ways to persevere. When faced with adversity, it's essential to remember that strength lies not in avoiding hardship but in enduring it, pushing forward, and never giving up—even when it feels like the world is against you.

RECOGNIZING YOUR OWN VALUE

Even in an environment where rejection and unfair treatment are common, it's crucial to recognize your own value. During my most difficult moments, I was treated as though I was less important than others. My relatives made me feel like an outsider, but I refused to let their treatment break my spirit entirely. External validation is not the measure of your worth. No matter how others treat you, it is vital to hold on to your dignity and believe in your intrinsic value. No one can take that away from you unless you allow it.

THE IMPORTANCE OF FORGIVENESS

At one point, I allowed anger and bitterness to consume me. I even contemplated revenge—like when I thought about burning my cousin after he threatened me. It would have been so easy to let my anger take control. However, I learned that choosing not to follow through with such destructive thoughts is far more powerful. Forgiveness is not a sign of weakness; it is a profound strength. Holding on to anger only damages your spirit.

Letting go of that bitterness allows healing to take place. It's one of the most significant steps toward personal growth.

EMPATHY FOR OTHERS

My experiences of hunger, rejection, and mistreatment taught me the importance of empathy. I know what it feels like to be unwanted and unloved, and that understanding has made me more compassionate toward others who are struggling. It's easy to perpetuate cycles of cruelty and neglect, but I chose to break that cycle. Instead of passing on the pain I experienced, I strive to be a source of empathy, support, and understanding for others facing similar hardships. It's through compassion that we can make a lasting impact on the lives of those around us.

THE ROLE OF A LOVING PARENT

My mother's support, despite her own immense struggles, highlights the critical role a loving parent plays in a child's life. Even though she couldn't always be there physically, her concern for my well-being and the comfort she provided during her visits were lifelines for me. A strong, supportive parental figure, even in the most challenging circumstances, can make all the difference in a child's life. If you are in a caregiving role, it is essential to be present and offer unconditional love, no matter how difficult the situation may be.

LIVING WITH INTEGRITY

There was a stark contrast between how my relatives treated me at home and how they acted in public, particularly in church. This hypocrisy revealed a powerful lesson about authenticity. True character is reflected in how we treat others when no one is watching. It's easy to put on a show of piety in public, but what truly matters is living with integrity—ensuring that your actions align with your values both privately and publicly. Integrity isn't about perfection; it's about being consistent and true to who you are.

STANDING UP FOR YOURSELF

Throughout my ordeal, there were moments when I had to stand up for myself, whether it was refusing to take out the urine that wasn't mine or confronting my cousin when he threatened me. These moments, though small, were crucial in teaching me the importance of assertiveness. Knowing when and how to stand up for yourself is essential to maintaining your dignity. Assertiveness is key to preventing others from walking over you, even in the most challenging situations.

THE POWER OF FAITH AND HOPE

In my darkest moments, it was faith and hope that sustained me. The hardships I endured would have been unbearable without the belief that things would eventually get better—whether through divine intervention or sheer perseverance. When life feels unbearable, faith in God, in yourself, or in the promise of a better future can provide the strength needed to keep moving forward. Hope, no matter how small, can serve as the guiding light through the most difficult circumstances.

HEALING FROM TRAUMA

The scars I carry, both physical and emotional, are reminders of the trauma I endured. But they also symbolize survival and the possibility of healing. Though the experiences were painful, they did not destroy me. Healing from trauma is a long, difficult process, but it is possible. Scars—whether visible or invisible—testify to our survival. With time, support, and self-compassion, it is possible to move forward and heal from even the most traumatic of experiences.

THE STRENGTH OF PERSEVERANCE

One of the most important lessons life has taught me is the value of perseverance. Even when food was scarce, when I was mistreated, and when fear gripped me, I never gave up. I endured countless hardships, but through perseverance, I survived. Perseverance is the key to overcoming life's challenges. No matter how impossible the odds seem, continuing to move forward, even if progress is slow, can lead to eventual success and survival.

You have within you the strength to be great, no matter what your background or social status is. It doesn't even matter the circumstances under which you were born. Your parent(s) may even think or say you were a mistake, but it is a lie. I was the product of rape, but none of that matters when you become born again. Those in Christ are a new creation. The old has passed, and the new has come. Struggles are not meant to destroy us; they are meant to make us stronger. The Apostle Paul sums it up beautifully, and I believe this is a fitting note on which to end:

"For I reckon that the sufferings of this present time are not worthy to be compared with the glory which shall be revealed in us." (Romans 8:18 - KJV)

Let these lessons from life built on a foundation of struggles be a reminder that you, too, can rise above your circumstances. You can endure, heal, thrive, and walk in the call and purpose that God has for your life.

Scripture's Encouraging Singles Parents

1 Peter 5:7 - KJV
Casting all your care upon him; for he careth for you.

Philippians 4:13 - KJV
I can do all things through Christ which strengthenth me.

Psalm 68:5 - ESV
Father of the fatherless and protector of widows is God in his holy habitation.

Isaiah 40:31 - KJV
But they that wait upon the LORD shall renew their strength; they shall mount up with wings as eagles; they shall run, and not be weary; and they shall walk, and not faint.

Psalm 147:3 - ESV
He heals the broken-hearted and binds up their wounds.

1 Peter 4:8 - ESV
Above all, keep loving one another earnestly, since love covers a multitude of sins.

Philippians 4:6 - ESV
Do not be anxious about anything, but in everything by prayer and supplication with thanksgiving let your requests be made known to God.

Philippians 1:6 - ESV
And I am sure of this, that he who began a good work in you will bring it to completion at the day of Jesus Christ.

3 John 1:4 - ESV
I have no greater joy than to hear that my children are walking in the truth.

2 Thessalonians 3:3 - ESV
But the Lord is faithful. He will establish you and guard you against the evil one.

Galatians 6:9 - ESV
And let us not grow weary of doing good, for in due season we will reap, if we do not give up.

1 Corinthians 13:13 - ESV
So now faith, hope, and love abide, these three; but the greatest of these is love.

1 Corinthians 13:4-7 - ESV
Love is patient and kind; love does not envy or boast; it is not arrogant or rude. It does not insist on its own way; it is not irritable or resentful; it does not rejoice at wrongdoing, but rejoices with the truth. Love bears all things, believes all things, hopes all things, endures all things.

1 Corinthians 2:9 - ESV
But, as it is written, "What no eye has seen, nor ear heard, nor the heart of man imagined, what God has prepared for those who love him"—

Romans 15:13 - ESV
May the God of hope fill you with all joy and peace in believing, so that by the power of the Holy Spirit you may abound in hope.

Matthew 11:28 - ESV
Come to me, all who labor and are heavy laden, and I will give you rest.

Jeremiah 29:11 - ESV
For I know the plans I have for you, declares the Lord, plans for welfare and not for evil, to give you a future and a hope.

Isaiah 41:10 - ESV
Fear not, for I am with you; be not dismayed, for I am your God; I will strengthen you, I will help you, I will uphold you with my righteous right hand.

Proverbs 3:5-6 - ESV
Trust in the Lord with all your heart, and do not lean on your own understanding. In all your ways acknowledge him, and he will make straight your paths.

Psalm 139:13-14 - ESV
For you formed my inward parts; you knitted me together in my mother's womb. I praise you, for I am fearfully and wonderfully made. Wonderful are your works; my soul knows it very well.

Psalm 139:13 - ESV
For you formed my inward parts; you knitted me together in my mother's womb.

Galatians 5:22-23 - ESV
But the fruit of the Spirit is love, joy, peace, patience, kindness, goodness, faithfulness, gentleness, self-control; against such things there is no law.

Matthew 19:26 - ESV

But Jesus looked at them and said, "With man this is impossible, but with God all things are possible."

Matthew 6:33 - ESV

But seek first the kingdom of God and his righteousness, and all these things will be added to you.

Psalm 127:3-5 - ESV

Behold, children are a heritage from the Lord, the fruit of the womb a reward. Like arrows in the hand of a warrior are the children of one's youth. Blessed is the man who fills his quiver with them! He shall not be put to shame when he speaks with his enemies in the gate.

Deuteronomy 6:6-7 - ESV

And these words that I command you today shall be on your heart. You shall teach them diligently to your children, and shall talk of them when you sit in your house, and when you walk by the way, and when you lie down, and when you rise.

Deuteronomy 5:16 - ESV

Honor your father and your mother, as the Lord your God commanded you, that your days may be long, and that it may go well with you in the land that the Lord your God is giving you.

James 1:27 - ESV
Religion that is pure and undefiled before God the Father is this: to visit orphans and widows in their affliction, and to keep oneself unstained from the world.

John 15:13 - ESV
Greater love has no one than this, that someone lay down his life for his friends.

Psalm 146:9 - ESV
The Lord watches over the sojourners; he upholds the widow and the fatherless, but the way of the wicked he brings to ruin.

www.ingramcontent.com/pod-product-compliance
Lightning Source LLC
LaVergne TN
LVHW051815080426
835513LV00017B/1961